The Customs House

ANDREW MOTION

First published in 2012
by Faber and Faber Ltd
Bloomsbury House
74–77 Great Russell Street
London WC1B 3DA
This paperback edition first published in 2013

Typeset by CB editions, London
Printed in England by T. J. International Ltd, Padstow, Cornwall

A CIP record for this book
is available from the British Library

ISBN 978–0–571–28811–3

10 9 8 7 6 5 4 3 2 1

for Kyeong-Soo

First one, then both sides of the meridian line:
my heart in the east, my west hand writing this.

Contents

3 SEVERAL LIFETIMES

1 LAURELS AND DONKEYS

Setting the Scene

Before I come to the trenches, let me tell you the village
is a ruin and the church spire a stump; every single house
has been devastated by shell-bursts and machine gun fire.

I saw a hare advance down the main street a moment ago,
then pause with the sun shining bright red through his ears.

Laurels and Donkeys

Afterwards, when everyone who suddenly burst out singing
has stopped again, Siegfried Sassoon settles back into the haze

of the old century. It is 1897, he is 11, and this is Edingthorpe
in north Norfolk. His mother, wearing her light purple cloak,

has packed herself with the wicker picnic basket, bathing gear,
and three sons into the long shandryman, drawn by a donkey,

which has been led round from the Rectory by the gardener.
There is a plan to take a dip in the river but, as the expedition

begins, Emily Eyles appears on the doorstep exclaiming
Madam has left without her sunshade after all. No matter.

When everything is quiet again, she closes it with a neat click
and the faintest creak of collapsing silk, then traipses indoors

where she falls to thinking about Mr Dawson, her young man,
who has saved for long enough to open his shop in the village

when they are married next year. 'White wings that never
  weary,'
she sings, washing up cups and dishes. By now the little party

has reached the village church, where the years become
  confused.
Siegfried clambers down without the others noticing, and leans

his leather elbows on the lych-gate. The carved gold lettering
  says
it was built when the war ended, in memory of a lance-corporal

whose father was rector here for 19 years and is buried nearby,
although the boy himself, having fought at Mons, Le Cateau,

the Arne, the Aisne, The First Battle of Ypres and at Hill 60,
drowned in the Transport *Royal Edward* crossing the Aegean Sea

on 13 August 1915. By peculiar chance it is 13 August today,
and in a moment Siegfried's younger brother will also be buried

at sea, after receiving a mortal wound on the Gallipoli Peninsula.
'Don't let the donkey eat the laurel,' their mother tells the children;

she knows it is poisonous. Laurels and donkeys. Siegfried agrees,
but will not ruin his afternoon, so picks a poppy and a cornflower,

lays them on the ground beside the lych-gate, then turns placidly
down the farm lane, over the style, and along the path that leads

through the meadow to the Rectory garden, and so to the river,
where in another short minute or two the others find him waiting.

An Equal Voice

We hear more from doctors than patients. However hard he tries, the historian cannot even the account, cannot give the patients an equal voice, because most of them chose not to recount their experiences.
– 'A War of Nerves', Ben Shephard

War from behind the lines is a dizzy jumble.
Revolving chairs, stuffy offices, dry-as-dust
reports, blueprints one day and the next –
with the help of a broken-down motor car
and a few gallons of petrol – marching men
with sweat-stained faces and shining eyes,
horses straining and plunging at the guns,
white sweat-clouds drifting beneath them,
and piles of bloody clothes and leggings
outside the canvas door of a field hospital.
At the end of the week there is no telling
whether you spent Tuesday going over
the specifications of a possible laundry
or skirting the edge of hell in an automobile.

*

There were some cases of nervous collapse
as the whistle blew on the first day of battle.
In general however it is perfectly astonishing
and terrifying how bravely the men fight.
From my position on rising ground I watched
one entire brigade advancing in line after line,
dressed as smartly as if they were on parade,
and not a single man shirked going through
the barrage, or facing the rapid machine gun
and rifle fire that finally wiped them out.
I saw with my own eyes the lines advancing
in such admirable order quickly melt away.
Yet not a man wavered, or broke the ranks
or made any attempt to turn back again.

*

A soft siffle, high in the air like a distant lark,
or the note of a penny whistle, faint and falling.
But then, with a spiral, pulsing flutter, it grew
to a hissing whirr, landing with ferocious blasts,
followed by the whine of fragments that cut
into the trees, driving white scars into their trunks
and filling the air with torn shreds of foliage.
The detonation, the flash, the heat of explosion.
And all the while fear, crawling into my heart.
I felt it. Crawling into me. I had to set my teeth
and steadied myself, but to no avail. I clutched
the earth, pressing against it. There was no one
to help me then. O how one loves mother earth.

*

One or two friends stood like granite rocks
round which the seas raged, but very many
other men broke in pieces. Everyone called it
shell-shock, meaning concussion. But shell-
shock is rare. What 90% get is justifiable funk
due to the collapse of the helm of self-control.
You understand what you see but cannot think.
Your head is in agony and you want relief for that.
The more you struggle, the more madness creeps
over you. The brain cannot think of anything at all.
I don't ask you what you feel like but I tell you
because I have been like you. I have been ill as you
and got better. I will teach you, you will get better.
Try and keep on trying what I tell you and you will.

*

The place was full of men whose slumbers were morbid,
titubating shell-shockers with their bizarre paralyses
and stares, their stammers and tremors, their nightmares
and hallucinations, their unstoppable fits and shakings.
Each was back in his doomed shelter, when the panic
and stampede was re-enacted among long-dead faces,
or still caught in the open and under fire. This officer
was quietly feasting with imaginary knives and forks;
that group roamed around clutching Teddy Bears;
one man stripped to his underclothes and proclaimed
himself to be Mahatma Gandhi; another sat cramped
in a corner clutching a champagne cork; one chanted,
with his hands over an imaginary basket of eggs, Lord
have mercy on us, Christ have mercy, Lord have mercy.

*

I could feel the bullets hit my body. I could feel
myself being hit by gunfire and this is what made me
sit up and scream. What I saw round me were others
walking with the bent and contorted spines of old age,
or moving without lifting their legs but vibrating them
on the ground. All equally unfortunate, filled with sadness.
Dead friends gazed at them. Rats emerged from the cavities
of bodies. Then trembling began, and losing control of legs:
you never dreamt of such gaits. One fellow cannot hold
his head still or even stand except with incessant jerking.
Instantly the man across the aisle follows suit. In this way
the infection spreads in widening circles until the whole
ward is jerking and twitching, all in their hospital blues,
their limbs shaking and flapping like the tails of dogs.

*

Naturally it can save a good deal of time if men,
before battle, have pictures from the Hate Room hung
in their minds of things the enemy have already done,
waiting to be remembered. Starving people for instance
and sick people and dead people in ones and heaps,
with bodies all bearing witness to hideous cruelties.
Compulsory mourning is no longer recommended
whereby the hospital confines a man for three days
alone in a darkened room and orders him to grieve
for dead comrades. But other cures must be attempted,
and in some cases men even wish to return to their duty.
See, your eyes are already heavy. Heavier and heavier.
You are going into a deep, deep sleep. A deep, far sleep.
You are far asleep. You are fast asleep. You have no fear.

*

I am quiet and healthy but cannot bear being away
from England. I have been away too long and seen
too many things. My best friend was killed beside me,
I have a wife and two children and I have done enough.
I thought my nerves were better but they are worse.
The first fight, the fight with my own self, had ended.
I may be ready to fight again but I am not willing.
I am in urgent need of outdoor work and would be glad
to accept a position as a gamekeeper at a nominal salary.
My best friend walked back into my room this morning,
shimmering white and transparent. I saw him clearly.
He stood at the foot of my bed and looked right at me.
I asked him, What do you want? What do you want?
Eventually I woke up and of course I was by myself.

The Death of Harry Patch

When the next morning eventually breaks,
a young Captain climbs onto the fire step,
knocks ash from his pipe then drops it
still warm into his pocket, checks his watch,
and places the whistle back between his lips.

At 06.00 hours precisely he gives the signal,
but today nothing that happens next happens
according to plan. A very long and gentle note
wanders away from him over the ruined ground
and hundreds of thousands of dead who lie there

immediately rise up, straightening their tunics
before falling in as they used to do, shoulder
to shoulder, eyes front. They have left a space
for the last recruit of all to join them: Harry Patch,
one hundred and eleven years old, but this is him

now, running quick-sharp along the duckboards.
When he has taken his place, and the whole company
are settled at last, their padre appears out of nowhere,
pausing a moment in front of each and every one
to slip a wafer of dry mud onto their tongues.

Beyond All Calculation

We left England before dawn, flying high and easy
across the Channel, then dropped into the worst of it
behind a farmhouse near Le Mesnil; forty or fifty men
were awaiting evacuation, so we dealt with them fast,

before hundreds of others began arriving from Gold Beach.
The yard was soon like the threshold of a slaughterhouse –
bloodstained uniforms, boots, caps and helmets and berets.
The interior of the kitchen and double-parlour is best left

to the imagination. Suffice it to say we would be kept busy
for three or four days straight through without any sleep,
but we had Benzedrine, and so did the stretcher-bearers –
willing but unseasoned boys who took it the hardest,

hesitating to lift their burdens unless they could turn
their backs. They became veterans that first morning.
Anyone would have done, watching the hands working,
seeing the orderlies giving blood, the wounds excised

then dressed as soon as the bleeding was under control
and limbs immobilised. When the break-out finally came,
with the men squeezed tight together in those deep lanes
and pressing towards the horizon, they found cattle dead

in the grazing on every side, their legs up stiff like toys.
No one had milked them; it was something that had been
forgotten. In the silence afterwards, ambulances appeared.
We climbed into these with our equipment and followed on.

John Buxton

Captain John Buxton, a prisoner of the German army
for all five years of the Second World War, examined
with precision and devotion the life of the creatures
around him, then chose as his one particular subject
the redstart, a small bird that in continental Europe

usually prefers the surroundings of human habitation
but in Britain is a secretive devotee of the wood-edge.
It is clear from his work that leisure, especially if limited,
is very much better used in the study of a single species
than attempting a general and comprehensive survey.

He began as he meant to continue: *I must be understood*
to refer only to my redstarts. My redstarts? The chief joy
of watching them is to prove they inhabit another world.
He ended as he began, after eight hundred and fifty hours
scrutinising a single pair between April and June 1943

near the left bank of the river Altmuhl where it flows
through the former valley of the Danube near Eichstatt.
Although no pair of birds has ever been watched so closely,
I feel that I know only a little of these strange creatures,
merrily busking about the pine trees that shaded some

two thousand of us, or perching on the wires that kept us
close. Their pink and silvery wings. The fragile pattern
of their songs and the ethereal sweetness of their actions.
What matters is: the redstarts lived where I could see them,
untroubled all day long except by their own necessities.

Matinee Idol

Hello Mother you will remember I always wanted
to be a movie star. Now they have encouraged us

to make this and promise it will be shown widely
in the cinemas at home; funny how things turn out.

I am well as you see and no small thanks to your cake –
the other fellows were very glad to share that with me.

Give my regards to Father and also to Nancy; tell her
not to worry. I am well as you see. Also give my best

to Uncle Eric and Aunt Betty, Steve, and everyone else
at the White Hart. To everyone you can think of in fact.

Tell them not to worry about me. I am well as you see
and will be home quite soon with everything forgotten.

That's my time up, so I shall say good-bye for the moment.
Here is Corporal Wagstaff with a message for his Mother.

Changi

For the funeral of Miss Jackson, a retired missionary
of the Methodist mission, our congregation was joined
by some from the women's camp. This was the first time

I had been part of a mixed group since captivity began
three years before, and hearing the voices of these women
I turned aside to inspect a troop of small yellow flowers

under a grove of rubber trees. I had never seen this plant
before coming to the Sime Road Camp. So far as I knew
it was the only species of wild flower to flourish there

in short turf, like the crocus at home. It had a green stalk
a foot high, and a head of three petals folded into a bulb.
I thought it must be an iris and have since confirmed that.

The Station at Vitebsk

Our town stood on the extreme limit of the world.
At the railway station, all the trains that drew up
to Platform One were returning home to Vitebsk,
and all the trains at Platform Two were leaving

Vitebsk. We swung between hello and good-bye
like the long brass pendulum of the station clock
that never helped me answer my question: were we
living at the beginning of the world or the end of it?

The waiting-room had a ceiling painted blue and gold
but the atmosphere was always tense with anxiety –
everyone was preparing to leave for somewhere else.
They might hear the bell ring three times and still

have to watch their train disappear into the distance
without them: the destination had not been announced.
All they could do then was settle down to wait again,
as if next time the Messiah would finally show himself.

My beautiful train roared, the boiler gulped flames,
and steam swallowed truck after truck of passengers.
We were travelling at last, losing the town in a cloud.
I felt I might have been going home after a funeral,

or setting out on my way to a funeral. Would there be
a place for me when I arrived, and faces I recognised?
Would the trees still be there – the deep forest I knew,
and used to feel breathing on me when I was a child?

The Korean Memorial at Hiroshima

There was hardly time
between the Peace Museum
and the bullet train to Tokyo,
but our hosts instructed the taxi
to find the Memorial to the Koreans.
Ten thousand Koreans, killed that morning.
You, being Korean, had to see it.

*

We had been crying in the Museum:
the charred school uniforms;
the lunch-box with its meal of charcoal;
the shadow of a seated woman
printed on the steps of a bank.
Everyone else was crying too.
We shuffled round in a queue,
crying and saying nothing.

Then we stood in the rain
squaring up to the Memorial.
A spike of rusty flowers
and a tide-scum of dead cherry blossom.
Five or six miniature ceremonial costumes
made of folded paper and left to moulder.
Pink. Pink and custard yellow.
You could hardly leave soon enough.

*

The taxi only just made it,
sputtering among black cherries
then stalling by the skeleton
of the one dome to survive the blast.

No need to worry about the train, though.
The trains in Japan run on time.

In two hours and fifteen minutes
we would see Mount Fuji,
cloud-cover permitting,
and the snow-cap like a handkerchief
draped over a tumbler of water
in the moment of suspense
before a magician taps his wand
and the tumbler disappears.

Now Then

It was not my war, but all the same
my father handed over the harness
of his Sam Browne for me to polish,
and his enormous boots. There was
no way I could ever make the toes
brighter than they were already.

*

Years later I was riding a train south
from Gdansk to Warsaw at 4.00 am.
The pine forest swarmed beside me,
lit by the gentle glow of our carriages
and sometimes by devilish icy sparks
which flew from our wheels at points.

*

Tell him about the smell, my mother said,
working hard on his buttons with Brasso
at the window-end of the kitchen table.
She meant the smell of Belsen, the first
my father had known of any such place.
He slowly shook his head. *I don't think so.*

*

The forest lasted for miles. Miles and miles.
Then for a second I saw deep into the heart
of a clearing: there was this swine-herd
lolling against the wall of his pine cabin
wearing the helmet of a German soldier.
And pigs rootling in the husky moonlight.

*

Why not? my mother continued her polishing.
Surely the boy is old enough to know history?
My father sighed: *Now then, you know the reason.*
That ended it. I kept my eyes down and attention
fixed on the long face looming in his toe-caps,
convinced my efforts would never pass muster.

*

Eventually I slept, dreaming through what remained
of the great pine forest of Europe, while my father
pounded along in the dark outside my carriage.
At Warsaw he fell away from me, but not before
passing his boots through the window and asking
would I mind giving them a last quick once-over.

After the War

My father is in the Territorial Army planning a rearguard
action.
On Salisbury Plain to be precise, the night before Annual
Exercise,
with a gale blowing.

He is sharing his billet with Colonel Sidgewick, who fought
beside him
in Normandy through the Falaise Gap, then across Germany
into Berlin,
where they demobbed.

Reveille is at 05.00 hours and they should be asleep but the
wind has other ideas,
accelerating over the Downs to make one last and
particularly fierce assault
against their hut.

The blow knocks Colonel Sidgewick's glass eye off his
bedside table,
which my father knows because he hears it hit the floor like
a marble.
Whereupon the Colonel

searches under the bed until he finds it again, rolls it around
his mouth
with a watery plopping noise, then screws it back into his
eye-socket
and makes an apology.

In Normandy

My father is confused. This is the bend in the lane
where Major Gosling on a recce for the regiment
found a Panzer tank blocking his way like an ogre
and, swivelling his eyes round to the back of his head,
reversed between these high stone walls at top speed.

It was Spring then but is Summer now, and the buds
of marigolds and buttercups in the fields on either side
have exploded in riotous jubilation. This is what puzzles
my father, turning on his heel just where the Panzer was
to hear the painful bee-buzz of the backwards engine

and see again how a bullet fired through the turret-slit
strikes the Major through the right leg below the knee
preventing him from driving, whereupon he stumbles out,
and hops a very long three miles back to find my father
and tell him everything he can expect to find ahead.

Demobbed

Sixty-odd years after the war ended my father returned
home. No one told me to expect him, and by the time
I reached the airport, crowds were already surrounding

the Arrivals gate. When an especially loud cheer went up
something told me it might be him, and I made an effort
to push through and enquire. Sure enough there he was,

with his square shoulders, ramrod back, and polished hair,
but wearing his city suit which surprised me, and at his side
my brother Kit. Kit obviously knew something I had missed.

In any case, they marched straight past me without so much
as blinking, while the crowd continued to cheer gratefully
and the brass band played Colonel Bogey, until my brother

wheeled aside and my father lowered his head to disappear
between those long yellow flaps that luggage goes through,
where I imagine he quite simply laid himself down and died.

The Minister

We flew Passenger to Kuwait, where our driver
ferried us to the military zone – they were boiling
tea at the check-point and waved us straight through.
The Freight Building, next to Military Departures,
was signposted in Arabic script with a translation

that read 'The Fright Building'. By the time our gate
opened I was weighed down by armour, and accustomed
to the American soldiers who milled round us lazily
but always called me 'Sir'. The Minister, a late substitute
and our raison d'être, was another matter. 'Fuck this'

was his verdict on officials who deemed our papers
not in order, and much else besides. We wasted a day
in the Meridian Hotel, then next morning set off again
for the airport. The fourth approach-road our driver tried
was the one without a blockade. 'Fuck that as well.'

The planes are in constant use, so when our Hercules
landed, the pilot left the engines running while the ramp
(which I recognised from shots of coffins coming home)
slowly lowered and stopped 18 inches from the ground.
It was a struggle to get on board, what with my luggage

and armour, but I found my seat, a narrow canvas bench,
next to a Major from 2 Para, who helped me with my belts
and ear plugs. There were no announcements. We taxied,
roared down the runway, and an hour later were in Basra
to take on an Iraqi general and his American liaison officer.

Eventually we reached Baghdad and started to corkscrew,
dropping tin foil to confuse the heat-seeking SAM missiles
before making an exceedingly low landing. When I jumped
onto the tarmac it crossed my mind I might break something,
but I bounced and walked on. Soon the Minister caught up:

What the fuck were we going to do now? Why the fuck
were we waiting in the open? Where the fuck was the Puma
that would take us to the embassy? 'Look over there', I said,
and a moment later we were lifting off again in a great hurry,
thrashing over the empty streets, firing flares when the pilot

received a message, which turned out to be false, that a missile
had locked on to us, and dipping close to the ground. The roofs
were wonderful, but the Tigris a disappointing chalky brown.
The Minister certainly thought so. 'Looks like a fucking drain.'
The surface whipped into little peaks as we crossed, and ahead

lay our landing pad in the Green Zone. We had arrived safely.
An hour later the Minister was in the bar practising his billiards.
'Hi', he said, when I approached with our schedule of meetings.
'Finally we seem to have got our fucking passports stamped.'
Then he leaned forward to concentrate on a difficult pot.

Losses

General Petraeus, when the death-count of American troops
in Iraq was close to 3,800, said 'The truth is you never do get
used to losses. There is a kind of bad news vessel with holes,

and sometimes it drains, then it fills up, then it empties again' –
leaving, in this particular case, the residue of a long story
involving one soldier who, in the course of his street patrol,

tweaked the antenna on the TV in a bar hoping for baseball,
but found instead the snowy picture of men in a circle talking,
all apparently angry and perhaps Jihadists. They turned out to be

reciting poetry. 'My life', said the interpreter, 'is like a bag of flour
thrown through wind into empty thorn bushes'. Then 'No, no', he said,
correcting himself. 'Like dust in the wind. Like a hopeless man.'

Op. Billy

We arrived at 05.30 hours in a bloody freezing Kabul Airport
with snow piled head-high either side of the runways,
then drove through town for ten minutes to ISAF HQ
where I had my first sighting of the actual Afghanistan.

This was people wandering across a dual-carriageway
and shepherds with flocks of straggly goats. Lots of goats.
I soon discovered we have a permanent goat detachment,
although at the time of writing, the elders from Sangin

have eaten the last residents. The Officer in Charge of Goats
(OiCoG) is presently in the process of resourcing more;
this operation, Op. Billy, is now a routine drill. The OiCoG
will drive to town in an armoured Land Rover with support

from associated personnel which, on reaching the bazaar,
takes up a defensive position around the livestock section.
The OiCoG then moves swiftly to the Goat Man and begins
negotiations. It is impossible to over-estimate the importance

of the local elders in dealing with troublesome provinces,
and so also of the need for a goat that finds their approval.
Fortunately the OiCoG is fully UN Goat Authority, Selection
and Screening (UNGASAS) trained, and within a few minutes

he will turn a goat on its back and make a thorough assessment.
Now that we have been compelled to forgo weekly camel racing
we are keen to procure two goats to initiate a similar contest.
Until that becomes possible, we make bets on the peak numbers

of diarrhoea and vomiting cases in camp. I have pitched for 75
but understand there are others who have gone as high as 140.
Good-bye for now. I am off to Death Row where I hope to sleep
soundly until 06.00 hours when morning prayers will wake me.

The Golden Hour

After major trauma, a certain percentage of victims will die
within the first ten to fifteen minutes. There is another peak
around the hour mark. And a third at the two-to-three day mark,
due to complications. We are not able to do much about the men
that are going to die in the first ten to fifteen minutes, so instead
we look to keep them alive during what we call 'the golden hour'.

For instance: one patient I remember had been in a blast situation
with no visible injury but we were not ventilating very well at all.
I put two openings in both sides of his chest with a big scalpel blade;
then I could stick my fingers in, and knew his right lung was down
because I could not feel it. However, I was now releasing trapped air
and the lung came up again. He had responded within the golden hour.

The Next Thing

My heart stopped but my hands kept working away.
I had a job to do. I threw the mortar down the barrel

and waited for the splash to come up, just waited.
It was bang on. The next thing was to extract our own –

but lifting a dead body from the ground is not easy.
The first must have weighed fourteen stone; plus radio

he was half a ton. I could not get him off the ground,
not properly, not enough to put him over my shoulder.

I thought, Jesus Christ! But I managed. It is only right.
Later on we met some elders from the village to discuss

the bodies of the enemy; they were shot up very badly.
Two were dressed in black – obviously foreign fighters

with grenades on them and mobile phones and notebooks.
Their skin was strangely waxy and suspicious-looking.

A third was wearing traditional dress with a red sash
and a turban that was off at the time; his eyes were sunk

and had rolled backwards – there was no brain left in there.
I dug a bullet out of the wall behind him with my bayonet

for a keepsake, and could clearly see the swirl on the casing.
Then I went down the valley to a stream with the other men

and we stripped to wash our hands and faces in the water.
After that we stayed firm and finished our clearance patrols.

The Vallon Men

On the gently sloping hill behind Norton Manor barracks,
home to 40 Commando, three trees, one for each marine,
have already been dedicated to the memory of those killed

during their tour of Sangin in 2007–8. A week ago today,
in bright November sunshine, fourteen more were planted
to commemorate those killed during the last six months.

'It was a very hard tour', said Gavin Taylor, aged twenty-
eight and a father of three. 'We have lost a lot of friends.
And we have seen a lot of things that are not ideal.'

Home Front

I *The Garden*

Near the end of life in my own body
I slept in a grove of mulberry trees,
with a mattress of soft sandstone
and warm breeze for my blanket.

I knew then I had crossed the brook
Cedron, and imagined strangers' hands
gathering the leaves that sheltered me
to feed silkworm, then silkworm them-

selves, working their miracle of change.
Gethsemane. I believe I said the word
aloud, and shortly afterwards the earth
was taken from me. When I awoke again

I had reached as far as the unsteady glass
of my front door at home. I could make out
my wife in pieces on the far side, stopping
in our hallway before she came to answer.

2 *Their Hats*

I knew we were in serious trouble when I looked
from the landing window and saw the two of them
together, their hats showing above the front hedge.

Our boy saw as well and I called out: Don't let them in.
But he thought it was Dad come back, so ran downstairs
and when they knocked he opened anyway.

3 *Landing*

It is difficult to imagine how beautiful a Hercules
transport plane can appear to be when cloud-cover
breaks and the home approach begins. The engines,
too: they start like a rumour, then become multitudes
at prayer, then a deep Amen. A most beautiful sound.

He detested the rain all his life although I adore it,
and was soaked through the instant I took my place
alongside him in our procession across the tarmac.
Dry sand would still have been glittering in his hair.
And in the corners of his eyes, his ears, more sand.

2 THE EXPLORATION OF SPACE

Waterloo Village

I looked down and your shoes did for me immediately
with that exciting ridge along their toes like a seam
which is normally hidden but was plain for all to see.

Then your face, your face when you turned towards me
for the first time and said 'Hello; you must be Peter',
to which I could honestly reply: 'Peter's my middle name.'

Brooklyn

When you stepped into Frankie's Bar for a coffee to go
I sat down to wait for you on the bench outside and saw
this man unlock the padlock on his bike, drag the chain
between the spokes with a tingling music, and disappear
in a confusion of miniature pale green helicopter blades
the wind set free from an ash tree arching over us both.
Then Frankie's door opened and you came back to me.

Montauk

Remembering how a wave made in Antarctica
preserves its shape for many thousands of miles
provided the water is fathomless and only starts

to die when the ocean bed shelves towards a beach
whereupon the crest still travelling unhindered
gradually topples forward ahead of the toiling feet

with no choice except to disperse the energy it kept
so long in store, we caught the train out to Montauk
and were content all day to watch the breakers there.

Cozumel

Small red handprints on extremely old boulders:
not blood of course but a very good impression.
Jagged flints. Altar-stones and a whiff of torture.
The jungle fiddling much closer as evening fell.

It is hard to say how pleased we were to hear
the starling back at our hotel. He knew by heart
the opening notes of 'Satisfaction (I can't get no)'
and sang them endlessly across the swimming pool.

Kwangju

The more you tell me, the more often it comes down
to the hard-pressed earth in your grandmother's yard.

Before she swept in the evenings she sprinkled water
as if she was sowing seed and the dust settled at last.

Afterwards nothing moved, not even the day-old chicks
stunned by the length of time it took the sun to disappear.

Pyongsan

When you had scoured the bamboo clumps and chosen
one bamboo right to make the handle, you split the next
into regular strips to be the hand and fingers of the rake.
They clawed across the hillside making almost no sound
but a quiver like sound travelled continually up your arm
into your ear while bamboo leaves were scraped together
and others fell to hide all trace of where your footprints went.

Holy Island

I am behind you on the mainland, leaning
on your shoulder and pointing with one arm
in front of your face at weightless cinders
which are ravens blowing above the island.

Boulder clay on the outcrops, and beaches
dotted and dashed with coal dust. Guillemots
whitening the cliff face. Small orchids clearly
still evolving in a downpour of Arctic sunlight.

How many years are there left to cross over
and show you things themselves, not my idea
of things? Thirty, if I live to the age of my father.
I cannot explain why I have left it as late as this.

Your black hair blows into my eyes, and I see
everything moving fast now. Weather polishes
the silver fields ahead. The ravens swoop down
and settle in the gorgeous pages of the gospels.

Orkney

We stopped for no particular reason I could see
beyond the bridge across a burn that hurtled
off the tops and into Harries Loch. But doubling
back into the twilight of the arch where grass

had made a secret lip to catch the water's breath,
we found the otter's feasting stone beside the track
that ran between one disappearance and the next.

Yong'In

When we had offered our gifts of sho-ju and dried white fish
on his altar, we took it in turns to bow down to your father,
pressing our foreheads to the earth before sprinkling his grave
with the sho-ju, and chewing a few strips of the fish, in company

with what we imagined to be his own quiet eating and drinking.
Later we drove back to Seoul along the valley, passing on the way
a gang of urchins bathing naked in the stream, which you also saw
when you came here the first time, thinking to leave him behind you.

Home Farm

The hare we disturbed in the yard of Home Farm,
that either limped ahead of us or bounded or both,

paused whenever we at our dawdling pace dropped
out of view, and so seemed to be leading us onward

past the deserted cattle pen and the cobwebby barn
stacked to the rafters with blue barrels of poison,

until we came to the wide gateway and the grazing
where it turned for one last look, leaving us a view

of tall grass shining in the wind which was beautiful
enough but now hid something we thought we knew.

Gaisford Street

1 *By Day*

When you wear those headphones I cannot hear
what music you are playing, just the sandal-patter
of silent keys.

In your third country now you are still travelling
and I am quite content to ride in your slip-stream,
although you insist I am what you came to discover.

2 By Night

Space roars past, and the time between planets
is exciting at first although soon I am homesick.
There is nothing else, I hear myself bellowing

into the infinite silence. Nothing and no one else.
Then I open my eyes and find everything the same
as it was before I began my travelling thank God.

You are still lying beside me with your bare feet
neatly crossed at the ankle, and your sleepy mouth
ajar in the way that reveals your delicious over-bite.

3 SEVERAL LIFETIMES

Ma-Ka-Tai-Me-She-Kia-Kiak

Several lifetimes
I worked in peace;
corn and turkey
were all depending.

Death is nothing:
the earth is not mine,
my hand's work
the shadow of cloud.

The Death of Francesco Borromini

for Peter Maxwell Davies

I

The architect Borromini, born Francesco Castello
in Bissone on the shore of Lake Lugano in 1599,
is dying in Rome as dusk falls on 2 August 1667
by his own hand. The point of his sword has narrowly
missed his heart, which by good luck or bad judgement
means he has time to summon a priest and confess,
also to recall what he must leave behind in the world.
To the confessor he freely admits it was impatience
at not having a candle to continue working in the dark
that persuaded him to point the sword against his chest
and fall upon it. Meanwhile in S. Carlino, his earliest
and still-unfinished masterpiece, the last sunlight burns
down through the eye of the dome like an angel arriving
to ask of those within: *Which of you has been my servant?*

2

In the hollow earth beneath S. Giovanni dei Fiorentini
a crypt as immaculate as a blown egg is the setting
for the most intimate and intense theatre of his death
and life. Someone, an already grief-stricken friend,
has left a pair of women's ballet shoes by the altar,
setting them neatly side by side and then departing.
The suggestion is that whoever it was understands
the weight of stone is the same as the weight of air
and, like a breeze blowing across a field of wheat,
will sway, curve, vault, bow, spin, stop and stand
with a visible force and leave the clear impression
of things by nature continually unseen and invisible,
or like a dancer, their white shoes printing the stage,
pounding it, even, but only to leap upwards and vanish.

3

S. Giovanni in Laterano is the next place of pilgrimage for his dying mind on its final inspection of everywhere that proves the thing it was. Medieval brick cries out beneath the new, austerely swaggering stone: *Mother and head of all churches in the city and upon earth.* Echoes crumple into the bays; they rise and multiply under the glamorous roof; they glide over the tombs where death is already ensconced and grinning. Each one is pitch perfect. It is like watching a parliament of crows at sunset, when the whole sky darkens with their arrival and, above and beyond their big racket of conversation, creaking wing feathers take complete control of the air as many thousands of birds swoop into their own places, where in a second they fall silent and will suddenly sleep.

4

While there is still light the eyes will operate, organising
now the flight of the mind into the Oratorio dei Filippini,
and the first example of a small but exceptional innovation –
namely, a balustrade on the upper floor based on triangles
formed by three concave arcs, set with the bulge appearing
alternately at the top, then the bottom. A quite novel shape.
The eyes rejoice in it, discovering here too is a kind of dance
and also a vantage point, an actual way through the marble
(white marble, streaked with grey-green, and coarse-grained
with shining crystals) to other examples of his close attention:
the cupboard in the refectory, for instance, with divisions
in which the Fathers kept their napkins; or the *lavamano*
in the vestibule, that takes the form of a large black tulip
with four petals standing, four spread out to hold the water.

5

Now it is the turn of the tongue, wondering how to speak
at last of S. Ivo alla Sapienza, the old university church,
where six bays represent the body, head, and four wings
of the bee, which symbolises the Barberini family, but also
the star of David, since the significance of stone continually
shifts its ground without moving. By much the same means
the confusion of Babel tongues blathering all over the tower
might also be a sign of wisdom, the gift of tongues, in fact;
or the very form of the vault – an immense marquee of light –
could be persuaded to reappear in a small tent-like silk cover
placed daintily over the tabernacle containing the sacrament.
There, the tongue wants to say and the brain too: *the meaning
of this is definitely that*. Then the incandescent brass bell tolls:
Never one thing. Never one thing. Never one thing. Never one.

6

In a glimpse of the afterlife, Borromini now claps his eyes
on the leading twentieth-century interpreter of his work,
the university professor, Surveyor of the Queen's Pictures,
Director of the Courtauld Institute and Communist spy
Anthony Blunt, climbing back stairs with special permission
to reach the roof of the Palazzo Falconieri. Here he finds
something not easily seen at street level: a concave loggia
crowned by a balustrade carrying Janus herms, whose two
faces in each case make a striking silhouette against the sky.
One looks over the tangle and rumpus of the city; the other
across the Tiber to Trastevere. As soon as the difference
is clear, all eyes that can turn now look in the same direction,
to see the long river carry away everything it still reflects
over the raking weirs and beneath a succession of bridges.

7

The last light is still sliding in a single weak column
through the dome of S. Carlino where he observed it
in the beginning, inscribed with fine curlicues of dust.
Borromini lies down and places his right eye exactly
under the beam, so it becomes a telescope to heaven –
except he is looking through the wrong end, and sees
only his young self setting out, complete with a plan
that matches his delirious heart to his meticulous brain.
There is no mistaking the brilliance of this, or the damage
he will do to himself. Jealousy and hypochondria. Rage.
Genius and more rage. Then the light disappears entirely.
With the sword run through my body I began to scream,
and so they pulled the sword out of my side and put me
here on my bed; and this is how I came to be wounded.

The Customs House

I kept to back roads on my way to the Customs House
but now I have arrived it is impossible to travel further
without paying export duty on the merchandise I carry.

They have torn down the old buildings and laid new grass
so the officers can see me approaching without difficulty
and prepare their long form with its infuriating questions.

Beyond them an efficient-looking factory and a white church
inside a white wall are almost smothered by prolific trees.
A jungle! I imagine dangerous animals might well live there

until I notice a man emerging with no obvious signs of fear.
He seems to be dragging a cart containing a chest-of-drawers.
If he were in my position, he would pay very heavily for that.

Of All the Birds

I *Magpie*

The magpie I like least,
who stole my wedding ring
thinking it was his

to hide it in his nest
along with glass and pins
and other shining things.

2 *Nightingale*

In the pine wood which grows on the sand dunes at Es Grau
rumour has it there are nightingales. Clematis we did find,

thick yellow and gold like honey turned back into flowers,
along with sea-holly and white lilies in the perpetual shade.

3 *Peewit*

Eventually I decided on the field
planted with winter wheat, although
the farmer would crucify me if he saw.

It was all down to my kite needing
space not possible in our valley,
although the ground was sodden,

and a trek to the centre hard going.
A peewit kept me company, broken-
winged and weeping, *Over here!*

tempting me into some act of violence.
Never mind, as long as her plan saved
the nest with its clutch of speckled eggs.

4 *Dipper*

One you showed me nested
on the far side of a waterfall,
another in what became a bubble
trapped when the current rose.

In all events the dipper marks
his passage with a flinty note
scraped against the softer sound
of everything that water does.

Then ups and quits his rock
to walk along the river's bed,
as if a living soul had found
a way to haunt the dead.

5 *Cormorant*

When it came to leaving
I went with the cormorant
flying well below the radar
and breasting the muddy lake.

Down the road was his double
at home on a rotting fence-post;
shabby wings hung out to dry
closed in the breeze of my passing.

A Glass Child

for Peter Way

On the landing in the dormitory above the classroom
in the Old Labs that science had long-since abandoned

two school friends as restless as I used to be took turns
with me, climbing on one another's shoulders and staring

through the trap-door everyone else had failed to notice.
What I saw there were the remains of a glass child: arms,

toes, legs, pelvis, torso, fingers, vertebrae, teeth and skull
all carefully preserved and stored in separate tidy heaps

which, thanks to the ash-coloured half-light and thick dust,
might easily have been confused with the facts of an attic

containing the forgotten treasure of test-tubes and pipettes,
alembic jars and other instruments of distillation and
measurement.

*

In the classroom a floor below that dormitory in the Old Labs
my teacher Peter Way broke into my head, and a light swung

over the lumber of knowledge I did not realise was mine.
He was dusting off the poetry of John Clare, just a name then

and nothing compared to the snipe and badger and flycatchers,
the trotty wagtails and ants I had already seen with my own
eyes.

I looked away from the pages, from his face by the blackboard,
and watched snow fall like thousands of pieces of torn-up
paper

over the trim grass and well-swept pathways of Paton's Quad.
What was I learning now? Peter Way had moved on to
describe

the journey out of Essex, where my parents had raised me,
and which John Clare left on foot, tramping from his asylum.

So much unkind weather and strangeness. I had lost my sense
of direction. I would surely live under a hedge and go hungry.

*

In the dormitory below the attic and above the classroom,
where every boy was given a wooden cubicle somewhere

between a penitent's and a prisoner's cell, I did my sums
each night to calculate how I had changed during the day.

Overhead in the attic I heard the child assemble himself
and pace softly to and fro across the creaking floorboards,

humming the high music that was like a finger rubbed
around the rim of a goblet. At an equal distance below me,

in the hushed classroom where a square of wooden desks
crouched in the moonlight, Peter Way moved very quietly

in rotation. He was expecting an answer from each of us,
but first we had to guess his question. When it was my turn

I could think of nothing he had not understood for years,
but I closed my eyes all the same and did my best to
concentrate.

Sunday

I have been sitting for so many years
on the cooler of the two pull-down lids
covering the hot-plates of the Aga,

its top has dented, which means it is like
the form a hare leaves when it has slept
in long grass, faint but unmistakeable.

And if not a form then a perch, a look-out post
from where I can observe you at your work,
clamping the battered green meat-mincer

tight to the edge of the kitchen table, pressing
down with what appears to be all the weight
in your thin left hand onto the beef chunks

to make them disappear, while with your right
cranking the handle that changes them into worms,
the white fat-threads magicked into soft rose red.

I have been hanging on every word you said,
but forget them when the one o'clock pips tell me
Forces Favourites is now over and *World News*

can begin, which brings you in your smartest shoes,
the shoes you wore for Matins in the village earlier,
to ask me, 'Well, are you ever going to move?'

Are You There?

My father and I shove back the furniture
to the four walls of the sitting room
then lie on the carpet wearing blindfolds,
his left hand holding my left hand.

Are you there, Moriarty? he enquires,
before tightening (I imagine) the grip
on his rolled-up copy of yesterday's *Times*.
There is only one possible answer to that.

I give it while rolling away to the side
but still clasping his hand, still in range,
and sure enough he manages a direct hit.
Now it is my turn, but the moment I lift

my weapon I realise there is no reason
to continue. I can tell from his stillness,
and the chill and stiffness of his fingers,
he has been dead for a good while already.

Passing

I was passing, so dropped in
to see what there was to see;

the narrow asphalt pathway
boasting a surprising fossil-life

of horse-shoes and tiny bells;
that c19 chimney-maker

with miniature brick chimneys
worn to smooth columns

either side of his green name;
the knapped flint church

with its metal watering-can
catching slow drips from a tap

overhanging the vestry step;
and nothing else moving

except my dead father –
slowly but definitely taking

my mother in his arms again,
allowing her present to end

at last in me, when he thought
there was no one else to see.

Gospel Stories

1 *That Which Is Conceived*

I was filled with regret
the moment
I lifted that sparrow's egg
then emptied it

by blowing very hard
but softly
into one pinprick and out
the other.

2 *My Father's Business*

My father's legendary fear of heights
an amazing fact when the cloudy skylight
opened to reveal the cloudy sky itself,

and he leaned or do I mean collapsed
against the chimney stack. I slipped off
my sandals and pattered light as rain

across the slates to straighten this one,
scrape the moss off that,
long after he began to call and call me back.

3 *Through the Corn Fields*

I am still walking the tyre-tracks
left behind by a tractor as it sowed
this crop of barley which now stands
at shoulder height either side of me.

When I hold out my arms like wings
I might just as well be flying at ground
level. I am the equal of each and every
hard little yellow seed that speaks to me

while I touch its whiskers with the tips
of my fingers and reminds me I am not
allowed to be here, I am trespassing,
although nothing on earth feels wrong.

4 *The Kingdom of God*

The last colour to see when the sun goes
will be blue, which now turns out to be not
only one colour but legion – as if I never knew.

5 *Hosannah*

A donkey sharing its stony field with a Nissan
somebody dumped years ago in the top corner
is still curious how this came to pass. As his lips
browse the cracked bonnet, and his weeping eyes

take in the long arm of a fig tree with many elbows
stretched across both front seats, a great multitude
of mosquitoes sways above the hollow of his back
acknowledging silence first one side then the other.

6 He Was the Gardener

Mr Manning, in fact, rising from the compost heap
where he has dumped from his barrow a full load
of dung and stable-straw and now turns to face me.

A few moments more and he will vanish for ever,
taking without permission in the pockets of his mac
every new-laid egg he could find in the henhouse.

The Visit

In memory of Mick Imlah

The very morning death took you away
you sauntered back through my window
with the black cat grace and nonchalance
which marked you out in the early days.
You were thinking maybe of a quick drink

in the Marlborough Arms: was I coming?
I was already there, thirty-five years gone
in a twinkling, but quick was not the word.
Six pints in, when it was no longer clear
whether our real subject was exactly how

London Scottish would catch Harlequins,
or whether Tennyson in fact might not be
Tennysonian at all, according to James,
or what the landlady might do after hours
when no one was looking but her Alsatian,

I understood there was life, and within life
there were games, which mattered because
they did not matter. It was your gift, Mick,
to know that from the start, and to keep faith
with the difficult but clever course it gave you.

To judge by the way your ghost then led me
round to my study and the present tense again,
with you still wearing the same brown brogues
and blue jeans, the same too-thick tweed jacket
and not breaking a sweat, nothing has changed.

I told you I was very glad of that. You lifted up
your head without saying good-bye, then stepped
over the threshold and strolled off with your hands
in your pockets, taking a view of the bald street,
the blank day, and black traffic grinding through.

The Natural Order

In memory of Philip Larkin

In the original photograph you included a foreground
with dozens of black bicycles chained to park railings
in a repeating-pattern that almost resembled bunting,

then decided to lose all that and make a separate print
which zooms in to explore a more luminous world
under the chestnut trees dominating the middle distance.

Sun destroys the interest of what's happened in the shade –
which is like *Blow-Up* but seen through your own eyes:
a whispering cave of branches rising to cathedral height

above a young man wearing a trilby hat. He has taken time
away from his work and settled into a deckchair to observe
what the entirely natural order of things might look like

before anyone turns them into a story. Here, for instance,
manifold kinds of half-light weave a leopard skin rug
where a couple could lie down together. There a small boy

carries his toy yacht towards the lake hidden from sight.
And there a woman in a sleeveless dress folds her hands
as she waits for footsteps that now seem less and less certain.

Whale Music

I

In the beginning I found it very difficult to believe
I was in fact alive. Was I a creature or a country?
I decided creature, and at the same moment also

discovered my voice. It was not so much a form
of communication with others as a way of proving
I was alone in the world, which has remained true.

Nevertheless, I continue to announce my presence,
speaking in tongues that create a definite shape
for everything I see, which is a glassy universe

without borders, crossing-points or territories,
let alone walls or doors, light or dark. Only currents,
fluctuations of temperature that mean almost nothing,

and sometimes, if I surface, the moon- or sun-light
in which I cannot fail to notice that by living slowly
I have become a catastrophic danger to myself.

2

When we abandoned our lives as gods or curiosities
we neglected to develop a sufficient appetite for safety.
The times you dashed at us with boats and harpoons

we might have dived down out of range but instead
stayed in clear sight and died. You could say therefore
the impression of wisdom given by my colossal forehead

is a complete illusion. Except as we gathered together
making only confused and feeble attempts to flee
we proved something you are still failing to understand.

3

I can confidently say I was never more amazed by my own size than the day Brendan the Navigator and his flock of monks managed a landing on my back in the midst of their isolation.

Presuming me to be an island, they then lit a fire of driftwood and said Mass in thanks for their Salvation. In their sleep later I ferried them to shallow water, where in time they went ashore.

4

When first recorded by listening devices my voice
was understood to be the ocean floor creaking
which is a means of calling it the loudest sound

of any creature that has passed through the world.
Other impressions I give are very gentle clicks;
a squeak like an immense underwater prison door;

clangs like the same door slammed hard shut
every seven seconds; and Morse code suggesting
human talk. This is the most recognisable sound

to you, and also the most mysterious since it allows
a perfectly good idea of what it is you want from me,
although how you might reply you know less well.

5

Now she is long-gone I can only speculate
and make that my existence. I heard her speak
once, a pressure through water like a wave

inside a wave, but never set eyes upon her.
The green chambers of my interminable palace
were deserted – emptiness succeeding emptiness.

It was the same when I dived down to the depths.
Was she there? Not so far as even I could make out.
The life I have without her is apparently complete

and doomed, but I deny this has made me a failure.
Like her, I am a prisoner of the splendour and travail
of the earth, but grateful to prove I have existed at all.

6

I have given you many long and tall stories to complete;
millions of soft lights; an excellent means of lubrication
for watches and other fine instruments; delicate bones

for corsets and strong ones for decoration and building;
the good edible meat of my body; and not to be forgotten
ambergris – which one scientist has said reminded him

of 'An English wood in Spring, and the scent when you tear
back the moss and discover the cool dark soil underneath'.
My last gift of all will be the silence of your own creation.

Fall

Now wind has died in the lime trees
I have forgotten what sense they made,
but not the leaf the wind dislodged
that fell between my shoulder blades.

Acknowledgements

Several of the poems in Part 1 of this collection, 'Laurels and Donkeys', are best described as 'found poems' – which is to say they contain various kinds of collaboration. Some use the words of others without much alteration, others edit and rearrange an existing text, and others combine existing sources with my own words.

The title and most of the content of 'An Equal Voice' are taken from the historian Ben Shephard's book *A War of Nerves. Soldiers and Psychiatrists, 1914–1944* (Pimlico, 2002). To this degree the matter of the poem is in the public domain. The poem is also indebted to *Shell-shock* by Anthony Babington (1997). Further acknowledgements are as follows: 'Setting the Scene' to a letter written by Captain Ted Wilson, quoted in *Weeds* by Richard Mabey (2010); 'Laurels and Donkeys' to *The Old Century* by Siegfried Sassoon (1938); 'Beyond All Calculation' to *Medicine and Victory* by Mark Harrison (2004); 'John Buxton' to *The Redstart* by John Buxton (1950); 'Changi' to 'Within Changi's Walls' by George L. Peet (2011); 'The Station at Vitebsk' to the Memoirs of Bella Chagall, quoted in *Chagall: Love and Exile* by Jackie Wullschlager (2008); 'The Minister' to 'A Visit to Iraq' by Gordon Campbell (unpublished); 'Losses' to *The Good Soldiers* by David Finkell (2009); 'Op. Billy' to Robert Mead, Ministry of Defence Press Officer, and Capt Dave Rigg MC, the Royal Engineers, quoted in *Spoken from the Front*, edited by Andy McNab (2009); 'The Golden Hour' to Lt. Col. Duncan Parkhouse, 16th Medical Regiment, quoted in *Spoken from the Front*; 'The Next Thing' to Cpt. Dave Rigg, Cpt. George Seal-Coon, Lance Corporal Daniel Power, Warrant Officer Class 2 Keith Knieves, Cpt. Adam Chapman and Ranger David McKee, quoted in *Spoken from the Front*; 'The Vallon Men' to 'The Marines of 40 Commando are Back from the Front' by Karen McVeigh, the *Guardian*, 18 November 2010.

Other varieties of 'found poem' appear elsewhere in the collection: 'The Death of Francesco Borromini' is indebted to *Borromini* by Anthony Blunt (1979); and 'Whale Music' to *Leviathan* by Philip Hoare (2008).

Most of the poems in Part 1 were first published by Clutag Press as a chapbook called *Laurels and Donkeys* (2010). Other poems in this book have appeared in the following: *Acumen*; *Archipelago*; BBC Radio 3; BBC Radio 4; *Brunswick Review*; *The Guardian*; *Ink, Sweat and Tears*; *Old City: New Rumours*; *Oxford Poetry*; *Poetry and Audience*; *PN Review*; *Poetry Review*; *The Reader*; *Rialto*; *The Spectator*; *Tellus*; *The Times*; *Times Literary Supplement*.

'The Death of Francesco Borromini' was commissioned by the Theatre Royal, Bath, as a text to accompany the Maggini Quartet's 2009 performance of the String Quartet No. 7 by Peter Maxwell Davies; 'Whale Music' was commissioned by the Deal Festival and performed there and at the South Bank Centre in 2011 with Matthew Sharpe and Sameer Rao.